CHEMISTRY

This dynamic series challenges you to change what you are doing, how you are thinking, and what you believe in order to rearrange, restore, empower, and impact your future in ways you've only dreamed about before.

This is not just information compiled from studies, books, statistics, but this is revelatory wisdom that comes from real life experience that has been tested and tried.

We firmly believe that the person who hears, studies, and applies the principles learned thru this series will be prepared to face the impossible and conquer it!

*"Coming Together is a Beginning
Keeping Together is a Process
Working Together is Success"*

Henry Ford

This book is dedicated to our parents,

Charles A. Moore Sr. and Vernelia M. Moore

And our grandparents,

Howard and Lula Mae Hines

Who combined were married for 121 years until separated by death.

Contents

Elements

An element can be described as a part or aspect of something abstract, especially one that is essential or characteristic.

A chemical element is each of more than one hundred substances that cannot be chemically interconverted or broken down into simpler substances and are primary constituents of matter. Each element is distinguished by its atomic number, i.e. the number of protons in the nuclei of its atoms. In total, 118 elements have been identified.

If you had Chemistry class in high school the first assignment was most likely learning the Table of Elements. The knowledge of chemical elements is fundamental for progressing in the understanding of Chemistry. It is the basic blocks upon which future information can be built. In the same way there are elements that are equally essential in building a successful marriage. These elements can stand alone or can be mixed in the same way as the chemicals on the element table.

The Element of THOUGHTS

Everything starts with a thought. Before it is formally spoken which gives it power the thought is formed. Thoughts formalize our belief systems and are the foundation of what transpires in our lives.

Thoughts have a presence (they come from somewhere). Although they are not visible, they are manifest. The origin can appear to be unknown but if searched out can be found in what has been allowed in the gates of our conscious. Some thoughts originate through family traditions that are both spoken and demonstrated while others are formed through what we hear and see on a day to day basis. Printed word through textbooks, newspapers, magazines, online articles, social media or websites shape our thoughts by alerting us and bring awareness to things we previously may have been unacquainted with. The spoken word whether through the news media, the words of a professor or conversation with a loved one and through the medium of song lyrics are quite powerful in informing our mind of different ideas and philosophies. Thoughts often linger in our minds for a while before action is taken. Some thoughts will stay in the same realm until they eventually fade away; but many will have a metamorphosis and take on new forms. Some thoughts become ideas and live on in the realm of dreams or "bucket list". Other thoughts move into productive cycles and become plans. Yet others become words. Both words and plans can turn into actions and both can have both positive and negative effects.

The element of thought joined with the knowledge and/or wisdom of God will always bring success. This combination will work prolifically in a life to bring about great accomplishment. However, thoughts combined with our own desires often lead to destruction. We must be wise regarding what we connect with in order to be happy and complete.

No matter what you determine to link your thoughts to be it positive or negative. Thoughts must be coupled with an AGREEMENT for action to occur.

The Element of AGREEMENT

Agreement is necessary for Action! There will be no act unless there has been some settlement or as some would say "shaking of the hands". The deed occurs because a decision was made to "do" something!

But it is what you agree to or on that determines the effect and affect the act will have in your life.

There is a story in Genesis 11 that talks about the inhabitants of the ancient land of Shinar. At this time the whole earth spoke one language. The people of the land determined they would *"build a city and a tower, whose top may reach unto heaven."*

The bible advises that the Lord himself came down to see the city and tower and in Genesis 11:6 said *"Behold, the people is one, and they have all one language; and this they begin to do: and now nothing will be restrained from them, which they have imagined to do."*

The element of agreement is so powerful that God himself had to come up with a strategy to destabilize its affect and effect. The effect was that agreement makes you unstoppable and because of their plan to make themselves a "name" outside of God would have had devastating effects for the future of mankind.

So, God set up a plan to assist mankind in not messing up their own future *"Go to, let us go down (agreement), and there confound their language, that they may not understand one another's speech".* [Genesis 11:7]

The wedding day is an outward sign of an agreement that two people have made to join themselves as one and to live out their lives in the element of agreement. Mark 10:8-9 (ESV) advises *"and the two shall become one flesh.' So, they are no longer two but one flesh. 9 What therefore God has joined together (has come into agreement), let not man separate."* Amos 3:3 (KJV) asks the question *"Can two walk together, except they be agreed?"* The answer is no! And therefore, the element of agreement is habitually attacked.

We must understand that the enemy is subtle and crafty. There will be no announcements that an attack is coming. You must be cognizant and attentive knowing an ambush is being set up consistently against your agreement.

The 2nd Voice

Destruction in a marriage comes from following the 2nd voice. The first voice spoken should be God's. As a couple (who has become one flesh) we come into agreement with what God says. The problem occurs when we listen to the 2nd voice. Be clear that complications to not occur upon hearing the 2nd voice but adhering to the thoughts of it. In the garden it was not until Adam took of the tree of the Knowledge of good and evil and "did eat" that everything changed! In the building of the Tower it was not until the moment the agreement is broken (due to their inability to communicate effectively) that the building progress stopped which resulted in their scattering abroad.

The 2nd voice is any that talks against the marriage covenant that was made. It is the voice that says, "it cannot come back together because it is too far gone." "There is no need in giving your all, when they are not giving their all."

The 2nd voice will always bring up the negative aspects of your marriage and not encourage the positive. The 2nd voice will not root for the, but always against it.

Be cognizant because the 2nd voice is never loud or boisterous, it is subtle. It does not speak in absolutes but is present to pose questions and find wholes to expose.

The 2nd voice can come from those who you deem

as "haters" but more often can be found from those who pose as friends. Many speak out of their own failed experiences resulting in sour and tainted outcomes. People allow their own situations to plummet to places that out of their control but still have a deep desire to determine yours. Be conscious of other's motives!

The 2nd voice will continuously speak. Your responsibility is to shut it down as soon as it is heard. You cannot give the 2nd voice allowance to disturb your gates. The strategy is for the negative speech to become a thought for your entertainment that leads to inner changing and thereby lead you down a path of no return. We must refuse to be fooled!

The 2nd voice will often come at a time when you are disgruntled. The enemy is smart enough to realize that you will not engage a voice speaking against your covenant when you are happy and feeling well pleased with your spouse. He is a skilled tactician and uses words wisely. He will not waste words or his time. The 2nd voice will be heard when you are trying to make a point that seems to go unheard or when you are frazzled by what you have just heard from your spouse. That is when you may hear "stop speaking to them! They will never understand you." The 2nd voice may also speak in broad accusations such as, "they have never really listened to what you say" or "they have never cared about what you think". It is the power of agreement that the 2nd voice desires from you. An agreement with the negative speech regarding what God has joined so that it <u>CAN</u> be but asunder. We must conduct checks of our spirit and soulical man and get them inline. You must reject the 2nd voice to keep division out of your marriage.

Agreeing to Disagree

Our goal is always agreement. As forestated there is nothing more powerful in a marriage than this element. However, you will find that sometimes we can only come into agreement when we agree to disagree.

Because a marriage is the merging of separate histories, thought systems, ideals and dreams it is important to understand the principal of submission. We have heard the scripture quoted often from Ephesians 5:22 *"Wives, submit yourself unto your own husbands, as unto the Lord"*. And have heard it used as a means of control. But submission is a word that represents an incredible showing of self-control, respect and management. Submission says that you trust your partners ability to lead. It shows that you believe that your spouse has the team's best interest at heart and will do what it takes to make you win! Submission is not about control, rather an expression of complete trust.

The commitment to submit does not necessarily mean that you agree with your spouse's opinion, idea or plan. It means that even if you disagree with the direction, blueprint, or strategy that you agree to allow them to lead.

When you pledge to submit you are not permitted to bring up the points in which you disagree. Agreement must reign and be the governor of the matter. Agreement comes first. Let its power supersede your opinion. When you do you will see that your attitude towards the matter will change completely.

The Element of FORGIVENESS

When it comes to matters of the heart, we tend to be spiritual hoarders. We gather and hold onto things that both bless us and hurt us. These experiences become our prize possessions and grow near and dear to our hearts formulating our future practices, involvements, and processes. We have all heard phrases such as "fool me once shame on you. Fool me twice shame on me" or "I love you, but I won't be a fool about you". These expressions are born out of circumstances where you put your heart and soul into assisting someone to be better, helping with a project or maybe loving someone who took it for granted or took advantage of your goodness.

Most of us can raise our hand when asked if we have had this experience. The outcome has the potential to be lethal and sometimes deadly; but it does not have to. What is the difference maker? Forgiveness.

Forgiveness defined is the action or process of pardoning or providing absolution or being exonerated. In our justice system this rite is given to a judge or president. According to Wikipedia by the end of his 2nd and final term on January 27, 2017 President Barack Obama pardoned 1,927 individuals. He issued more commutations of the past 13 presidents combined.

We have the power to grant pardons in our marriages by using the element of forgiveness. Using this element should be a daily practice.

Rid yourself of clutter

People who gather believe that the items have significance and typically associate people, places and things to them. When asked to get rid of the items the excuse often given is that someone special to them gave it to them. Or it reminds them of a special time in their lives. We have a few plants that were obtained at the funeral of our dear uncle and our desire is to have them with us whithersoever we go as we associate the plant with good memories of him. The difference between the plant and clutter is that the plant is benefitting us as well. House plants help to clean indoor air by absorbing contaminants, increasing humidity and generating oxygen. This works in turn to decrease stress, exhaustion, sore throats and colds. Clutter works in an opposite way. Lots of extra "stuff" makes it harder to clean resulting in increased dust. Extra dust triggers allergies and cause symptoms like sneezing, wheezing, and itchy eyes. According to research clutter has adverse effects on your mental and physical well-being as well. It can leave you feeling apprehensive, worried, and disheartened. Some studies have shown that cortisol (the stress hormone) levels are higher in people who have a cluttered home. [*Pervagon*] Clutter can also cause you to feel embarrassed and force you into seclusion leaving you isolated and lonesome.

As you can see removing clutter is highly commended in the natural sense and is advantageous to live your best life. This is equally prescribed regarding your marriage.

Holding on to old arguments, past hurts and feelings associated with wrong will not leave your marriage in a healthy space. It is futile to rehash bitter words and out of control scenarios. If it hurt you while it happened, it will hurt again in the reviewed version. The healthy thing to do is to let it go. Banish it to the past and allow it to only live as a distant memory. The bible advises us that love "*keeps no record of wrong*". Those in my generation should still remember a device called a record player. We loved this equipment that allowed for the distribution of sound from a LP or album. This of course was before the days of portable radios, boom boxes, Walkman, MP3 players, iPods and now smart phones. We would come together and listen to the beautiful voices or spoken word of our favorite artists. Because you had the album on hand you could listen to your favorite song whenever you wanted to by walking over to the device and lifting the needle and putting it down in the same space. When the record player became obsolete many people threw their records away. They kept no records because they no longer had use and would become clutter. We must do the same in our relationships. We must throw out the record of wrong. Do not hold on to it because it makes you feel superior to your spouse. Do not hold on to it to use as fuel when they have done something else. Do not hold on to it to prove how right you are. Let it go and free yourself from the soul tie that keeps you connected to history. Why? Because your future is at stake and is so much more important. The past cannot be altered but the future is yet to be established.

Be aware of your tendencies.
Let every man examine himself.

We tend to blame everyone else for the calamities in our lives. Most people have a hard time accepting responsibility for the situations they find themselves in. Someone told us that calamity is equal to failure instead of an opportunity to start again.

We have been made to believe that blocks are meant to stop us and cannot possibly be used for building material. We look at disaster as only devastation and not as a dream starter; therefore, when these scenarios present, we must find someone else to be liable.

Perspective is Everything!

You can see it as:
A Block or **Building Material**
Calamity *or a* **Chance** *to start anew*
Sheltered *or* **Safeguarded**
A **Disaster** *or a* **Dream Starter**

Adjust your Vision!

The truth of the matter is 90% of what we deal with in life is brought on by ourselves or more specifically how we perceive a situation. Perception is everything. Proverbs 23:7 advises "*As a man thinketh in his heart, so is he*". If you see yourself as a defeated person, someone who people look down on, unworthy of love, disagreeable, or a victim then everything said or done to you will fall into those categories no matter the intention of the other person.

We made our children learn and recite a poem that has resonated with them throughout life and reverberates with us today. It speaks of what you think about yourself and the results of what you think. We believe that it would be of benefit to you as well and have inserted it for your reading pleasure.

Thinking
by Walter D Wintle

If you think you are beaten, you are;
If you think you dare not, you don't.
If you'd like to win, but you think you can't,
It is almost a cinch you won't.

If you think you'll lose, you've lost;
For out in this world we find
Success begins with a person's will
It's all in the state of mind.

If you think you're outclassed, you are;
You've got to think high to rise.
You've got to be sure of yourself before
You can ever win the prize.

Life's battles don't always go
To the stronger or faster man;
But sooner or later the person who wins
Is the one who thinks he can!

We have heard someone express their love and respect for their spouse describing how smart, beautiful, and generous they are and was astounded and confused to hear the partner describe that they heard something totally opposite. This is when we determined the necessity of each individual checking ourselves and our viewpoint before moving forward. Perhaps it is not you, it is me!

Women have been instructed for several years of the importance in doing self-breast examinations at least once a month. Statistics show that at least 40% of breast cancers are noticed by women who have found a lump or malformation during their own exam. Early prevention can prolong life by allowing for early treatment. The steps for the self-examination include examining yourself from two different positions first while standing looking in a mirror and while laying down.

We can use this same process for evaluating ourselves. First, we should set a time to reflect each month. It should be a predetermined time so that we are not affected by external stimuli that may happen and could alter our view. We must ask ourselves:

- Has anything changed from last month?
- What have I done to help our situation?
- What have I done to hinder our situation?
- What have I done to bring hope?

Forgiveness is the key to Longevity

Most traditional wedding vows include a phrase that speaks to longevity. We promise to love, honor, and work with our spouse "till death do us part" or "as long as we both shall live". When we are filled with happiness and glee from the wedding day forever seems like a short time and we imagine that even forever is too short of a timeframe to spend with the one we adore. However, as time goes by there are times that you will wonder if you can make it through the night with your spouse. Without the element of forgiveness there is no way to move through the night seasons and get back on track to forever. Research suggests that harboring feelings of disloyalty may be linked to high blood pressure which can ultimately lead to stroke, kidney or heart failure, or even death in the natural; so, please imagine what it is doing to your soul.
True forgiveness requires repentance, but not as you think. Most believe that the spouse that has committed the offense should repent and "turn from their wicked ways". If the person has committed a sin against God and broke their marriage vows, they should repent to God and ask their spouses forgiveness. However, repentance is also necessary for the offended.
Repent is taken from the Greek word Metanoia which means a transformative change of heart. A transformative change is required to approach the offending spouse in the correct way and move the marriage forward. Without true repentance it is

hard to see your partner outside of the film of disgust or blight that formed in your eyes when they upset you. Repentance is always personal and is about freeing yourself from the pain and hurt. Repentance allows your view to be changed. When you see different you speak different. When there are no obstructions in your viewpoint you can see further down the road and it makes for a pleasant and easy drive.   And by the way, God requires it!

The Model Prayer

Matthew 6:6-15
*6 But thou, when thou prayest, enter into thy closet, and when thou hast shut thy door, pray to thy Father which is in secret; and thy Father which seeth in secret shall reward thee openly. 7 But when ye pray, use not vain repetitions, as the heathen do: for they think that they shall be heard for their much speaking. 8 Be not ye therefore like unto them: for your Father knoweth what things ye have need of, before ye ask him. 9 After this manner therefore pray ye: Our Father which art in heaven, Hallowed be thy name. 10 Thy kingdom come. Thy will be done in earth, as it is in heaven. 11 Give us this day our daily bread. 12 And **forgive us our debts, as we forgive our debtors**. 13 And lead us not into temptation but deliver us from evil: For thine is the kingdom, and the power, and the glory, forever. Amen. 14For if ye forgive men their trespasses, your heavenly Father will also forgive you: 15 But if ye forgive not men their trespasses, neither will your Father forgive your trespasses.*

No need to add to the scripture. It is simply stated

that you cannot ask God to do anything for you that you are unwilling to do for others.

The Element of LOVE

So much has been said about love. It has been written, sung and talked about since the beginning of time. It elicits various emotions and causes both laughter and tears. It brings hope and promise of a new day. It fills hearts and brings joy.

On the contrary the lack of love empties a heart of elation. It leaves a longing and desire that needs to be filled. When love is lost it plummets happiness like a balloon that someone has popped with a pin.
Everyone wants to love and be loved, but few understand what real love is.

The bible tells us that God is love and in 1st Corinthians 13 Paul provides a description of how love operates.

TABLE of LOVE

Love never gives up	Love cares more for others than for self
Love doesn't want what it doesn't have	Love doesn't strut,
Love doesn't have a swelled head	Love doesn't force itself on others
Love isn't always "me first"	Love doesn't fly off the handle,
Love doesn't keep score of the sins of others	Love doesn't keep score of the sins of others
Love doesn't revel when others grovel	Love takes pleasure in the flowering of truth
Love puts up with anything	Love trusts God always
Love always looks for the best	Never looks back, But keeps going to the end
Love never dies	

Above All

The topic of love is inexhaustible. So, we want to narrow our discussion of this essential element to a few important focuses. The first is found in 1 Peter 4:8 (KJV) "8 *And above all things have fervent charity among yourselves: for charity shall cover the multitude of sins.*" This scripture is expressed in more detail in the The Passion Translation (TPT) "8 *Above all, constantly echo God's intense love for one another, for love will be a canopy over a multitude of sins.*"

When the instruction starts with <u>above all</u> we know it is important. The scripture advises us beyond all of the other great things we should allow love to work in and through us such as, exhibiting patience and kindness in our relationship and including putting down envy and boasting, that we should echo God's concentrated, penetrating, extreme and unconditional love.

An echo is not just the reverberation of sound coming back to our ears following soundwaves. It is a close parallel or repetition of an idea, feeling, style, or event. God showed his incredible ability to love us when he gave his only son as a ransom for us! His love motivated Him to make the ultimate sacrifice to purchase our salvation and free us. He is asking us to do as He did. To love with such fervency that we are willing to sacrifice our all for the wellbeing of our spouse! It is not until you can love in this manner that you have entered into loving like God.

In the marketing arena the "echo effect" is when a slogan or jingle gets into everyday talk. Advertisers love to get people to incorporate slogans into regular conversation because they no longer need to funnel millions of dollars into commercials and ads because we are doing the promotion for them. We must step into the echo effect of loving our spouse like God loves us until it becomes our norm.

How do you take this spiritual principle and work it in the natural? You speak it and believe it! God's plan for you is to love each other for life. His plan should become your goal.

All Things

1 Corinthians 13:7 advises that "*love bears all things, believes all things, hopes all things and endures all things.*"   All means to the whole extent of; in total. All means all.
The first thing that comes to mind is that this is a ridiculous notion that is not humanely possible. How can anyone carry, endure and support ALL things? Particularly lying, cheating, disrespect? The word tells us that love bears ALL things it did not say that you had to carry, endure and support them. But we understand that a heart of love is the bridge to assist us in bearing the many things that may attack our relationships.

True love is not emotion based it is spiritual. We have all seen parents who have experienced the heartache associated with a child who rebels, constantly lies, is disrespectful, steals, or even physically abuses their parents and wonder how the parents remains sympathetic, compassionate, and helpful. Perhaps you are that parent.
Any parent with natural affections for their child wants to see them through the storms of life and will do ALL they can to help them get to a better place. Why? Because the love is a spiritual bond not based on temporary feelings. It is eternal.

A marriage bond should be the same. The promise to love for a lifetime for better or worse unfortunately may include the very worse. But, God kind of love can bear it. We are not condoning abuse of any kind nor do we pardon the

breaking of the vow or missing of the mark that Christ set for us. We are simply making the point that God kind of love is like a Timex watch. It can "take a licking and keep on ticking".
We must determine if we love our partner with agape love or something more earthly.

We all want someone to believe in us. We want someone who will back our ideas and champion our dreams. We want someone to say "I know it seems outlandish, irrational and close to impossible, but I believe YOU can do it! Our men want to hear us say "I have faith that you can lead our family and always do what is best for us. I believe that you will protect us with all the skill, determination and fight that you have and that you will make sure we are never in lack". Our women what to hear us say "I believe that you are my provider and have faith that you will take care of me, stand beside me and assist me in every effort that I put my hands to. That you will trust me to love you in the way you need to be loved and to satisfy your requirement to be desired and cared for.
We both want to hear that "we believe each other

> **MARRIAGE MINUTE:**
>
> Find a scripture that speaks of God's great love for us and turn it into a phrase that you can echo that expresses his desire for your marriage.
>
> **Example:** We call each other **EDC** & **LL**.
>
> **EDC** stands for **Everyday Choice** and **LL** for **Lifetime Love**. Each time we use these phrases we reiterate our commitment to love each other as God loves us!

to put our union first and foremost above everything and everybody including our children; that nothing is bigger than us and that we can and will have a happy and empowered marriage."

If you take away hope, there is no path forward to faith. Hope is vital. It is one of the things that remains with faith and love. It is not as great as love, but it is in the top three.   Hope gives us something to hold onto. It is the extension of a hand when you have fallen. It is the strong embrace when you are devastated, and it is hints of sunlight across the horizon when the night has been long, dark and winds tumultuous. When hope is gone, we descend; but when hope arises, we ascend. Hope in a relationship is the fuel that keeps it moving forward. It is the oil the keeps the engine running smoothly and is critical to make it run. Love hoping all things is so powerful. It means that as a couple we hold onto possibility! It suggests that we understand there are always options and that we see opportunity in every obstacle, triumph in every trial and deliverance in every disorder.
 Hoping all things leads directly into enduring all things. When you never give up hope then you embrace the fact that come hell or high water, chaos and calamity, disruption or destruction our unit is going to make it through to the other side of it, intact! Endurance requires a firm and fixed mindset. It is concentration at its best. It requires an unyielding stance and an irreversible commitment. It takes an understanding that we have merged into one unit and are better together!

Love is the most indispensable element in the CHEMISTRY of marriage. It is the foundation of every other element and blends smoothly although it does cause the chemical reaction of an explosion. However, this explosion does not cause damage, rather the total opposite it is an eruption of pleasure, satisfaction and peace!

COVENANT vs. MARRIAGE –Blurred Lines

While Chemistry is an exact science made up of established variables the words that we use to describe a union between couples have become blurred in terms of our actions and responses.

In modern society we use the word marriage to describe the coming together of two people.

The word "Marriage" did not originate in the Bible. The word marriage derives from the Middle English word *mariage*, which first appears in 1250-1300 CE. Marriage is described as the legally or formally recognized union of two people as partners in a personal relationship (historically and in some jurisdictions specifically a union between a man and a woman). However, the word marriage was used in Hebrews 13:4 advising that it is honorable. *"4Marriage is honourable in all, and the bed undefiled: but whoremongers and adulterers God will judge."* The writer expresses that the concept of marriage is righteous. It is principled and admirable as this institution is the expression of what God started in Genesis. Genesis 2:24 *"Therefore shall a man leave his father and his mother and shall cleave unto his wife: and they shall be one flesh."* Unfortunately, we have seen in our nation and many around the world that the definition of marriage can be voted and changed by law; but what God instituted, covenant, is totally different!

The bible speaks of Covenant. Covenant is described as a solemn compact or agreement made between people, groups or tribes. Covenants were binding and once written, the covenants were not to be altered or annulled. There are covenants in scripture that God made with man. These covenants fall in the classifications of provisional, absolute, and conventional. The marriage covenant falls into the classification of absolute. An absolute covenant is made with no strings attached and will be kept regardless of one party's devotion or disloyalty.

The intent of a Covenant of marriage is to form a union of a man, woman AND God in a triune agreement governed by the Word of God and the power of the Holy Spirit. Covenant is blood covered. You know you are in covenant when the power of God seals two spirits as one and the divine DNA transforms them into one.

Marriage is naturally formulated while Covenant is spiritually formulated. We have set down with couples for counseling who advised that love was not a reason for their coming together. They advised that they wanted to be married for the tax benefits. Others have expressed other financial situations that made a union warranted for them.

As most vows say, "marriage should not be something that is entered into lightly but advisedly." However, because it is a matter of law it can be accomplished if a license has been filed and someone is willing to perform the ceremony.

Legally, a marriage can also be dissolved with the filing of forms and payment of money.

Covenant is on a whole other level. The terms of a covenant cannot be reconstructed or rescinded. An unconditional covenant says that the parties will abide strictly by the conditions of the covenant through it all. Abiding by the covenant is living life together on God's terms. It takes no account of the trends and

COVENANT	MARRIAGE
Covenant is a divine contract	Marriage is a government contract
Covenant Upholds the Laws of God	Marriage upholds the laws of state

problems of the day. In fact, covenant does not look at what the next-door neighbor, brother, sister, cousins or parents are doing. The terms are set to love and honor your covenant partner for life. The covenant leaves no room for any influence from anyone outside of the ones participating in it. It advises that leaders, loved ones and mentors should be left and there should be a grasping and gripping to the partner. Clinging means to hold on, attach to, hang in there. This is the description of how to stay in covenant. It is further documented in Ephesians 5:33 that we should never engage with the less.
"Nevertheless, let every one of you in particular so love his wife even as himself; and the wife see that she reverence her husband." Entertaining less is a fail-safe path to breaching the covenant. We should always go for executing more! More is

looking past shortcomings, weaknesses and mistakes to remain committed to the covenant. More is being steadfast in placing the covenant before your emotions. More is not searching for better but respecting the value of the covenant.

Covenant applies a combination of love and respect and the many children of this couple that include patience, thoughtfulness, compassion, tenderness, and honesty.

Covenant uses all the elements of CHEMISTRY to elevate the couple to a Complete, Happy, Empowered Marriage.

We're a team

CHEMISTRY is all about building your team and doing the work. Teamwork takes communication, cooperation and coordination. Teamwork may mean putting the needs of others before yours. Teamwork always requires seeing the big picture and doing what is best for the group and not the individual members.

Teamwork says……

"Whatever you lack, I got you. We will balance each other.
Minor setback? We'll make a major comeback.
Bad day? I promise you a better night.
You need support? I'll be your backbone.
I'll keep you motivated and at the top, ALWAYS!
Let's promise to always appreciate each other.
Let's remain consistent.
You don't ever have to doubt my loyalty.
You got me, I got us!"

CHEMISTRY is not hard. But it does require effort. It takes specific elements in confluence together to produce an effective reaction.

You have been gifted with information to expose the limitations in your marriage and keys to cause a healthy explosion of enjoyment and pleasure for years to come!

The key to a long-lasting marriage that never ends in divorce is:
NEVER LEAVE!

Authors Page

Kirk and Jotwyla Moore have been married for over 25 years. They firmly believe that empowering and bringing restoration to marriages is a part of their purpose.

The couple hosted the CHEMISTRY Marriage Conference for many years and has counseled many couples over the years.

They are the Pastors of Restoring Life Ministries and provide oversight to the Maximum Impact student organization on the campus of West Virginia University.

Mrs. Moore is the author of several books including *The Encounter, A Certain Woman Personal Application Guide to Living Life Without Doubts*, and *Devotions for the Seasoned Woman.*

Get ready for the next volume of CHEMISTRY. There is more to come!